LET THE BLIND HORSE LEAD

LET THE BLIND HORSE LEAD

*Forty-nine Poems
and One Prose Poem*

KIMBERLY KAYE ESTERAN

Lilith House Press
Mentoring Women Authors. Your Voice Matters.

Copyright 2022 by Kimberly K. Esteran

All rights reserved

No part of this book may be reproduced, scanned, or distributed in any form without the written permission from the copyright holder. For more information, please contact the author. www.Kimesteran.com

ISBN 978-1-736-9673-5-5 (softcover)
ISBN 978-1-7369673-6-2 (E-book)
Library of Congress Control Number: 2022901647

Cover and interior design: Jane Dixon-Smith/jdsmith-design.com

Editor: Jane Kuhar
Illustrations: Jordan Kaye Davis
Author photography: Eric Esteran
Illustrator photography: Mark Richards

*For Bernadette and John Spillane
who dream dreams and make them real*

*and all the people and animals at the
Happy Dog Ranch Foundation
where miracles happen daily*

Thank you

Happy Dog Ranch Foundation: Rehabilitating Horses & Farm Animals; Educating and Healing People. We strive to connect humans with animals in a safe and nurturing environment where love and understanding will flourish. A Place to Heal is the title of a short documentary on the website, www.happydogranch.org

One hundred percent of the proceeds from this book go to support the Happy Dog Ranch Foundation. If you would like to learn more about them, please visit their website.

Rainbows

*When you live at the bottom of the rainbow,
do you see the colors?*

Or, simply live in a beautiful world?

Or, perhaps, not notice anything at all?

~Kimberly Esteran

Contents

Forward	1
Introduction	3
How Do Trees Decorate Their Toes?	7
Today ...	9
Where the Poems Live	10
Isn't It	11
Giggle Back to Green	12
A Poem, A Prayer, A Promise	13
Sacred	14
Now	16
A Little More Rose	19
How Many Times?	21
Simple	22
Being Present	23
Too Much Thinking	24
On Grace and Waiting	27
Please. Amen.	28
The Practice Before the Practice	29
June, The Month of Perfect Days	30
One More Thing	33
Fresh Mountain Air	35
The Wisdom of a Thousand Years	36
The Fall	38
Summer Solstice	40

Day Three	43
Stones and Tears	45
Holding Up a Mountain	46
Energy	48
A Daily Reminder	49
The Knife	50
Softly	53
Count By Touching	54
Good-bye Stories	56
Open My Mind	57
Cookies	59
The Apple Tree	60
Griffin Dreams	62
Long and Deep	64
Vitality	65
secrets	66
Thoughts on Surrender	67
There Is a Sweetness in an Old Dog's Joy	68
Walking Trees	70
In Your Eyes	71
And This …	72
Musings from the Stall	74
I Didn't Know	76
Tough	78
These Words	79
Let the Blind Horse Lead	81
Scatter Me	83
Epilogue	85
Listening to the Horses	87
With Gratitude	89
About the Author and Illustrator	90

Forward

~by Jeffrey Ritter

Serenity. Think of it not as a state of mind but, rather, as a destination, a multi-dimensional space in which you can find yourself, aware through each of your senses that all which surrounds you is wondrous. And you exist there. You belong there. Embraced.

In this third published collection of her poetry, Kim invites you to join with her heart and, in the silence and pauses between the words and phrases, witness the beauties of our world as she sees them, not those which stand large and monumental, but the shimmering jewels which are small, intimate and often overlooked in the blurs of our own velocities through life. Courageously, she welcomes us into where she finds serenity—shaped by personal, authentic, and vivid portrayals that demanded her to be fully present or she would perhaps have missed them.

Poets believe a book of their work can be organized, structured from a beginning to an end with purpose. Perhaps. But as you explore these pages, the brilliance of how Kim sees her world is the realization that there is no proper structure required—indeed there is no suitable starting point or end point. Instead, what emerges is a glorious sense that all of the parts fit together to construct and define a space where she finds serenity. So, I encourage you to wander, skip around, abandon conventions or order and, perhaps, defy the poet's design. In doing so, the breadth and beauty of this collection emerges with a quiet force, each poem seducing you back to visit again its words, and phrases, and the spaces between them where insights and wisdom reside.

As you meet her companions (both those with two feet and four), the passions she expresses with them, and the lessons she learns from them, Kim softly invites each of us to do the same—to observe our own worlds with due attention to the shimmerings, to be still enough to bear witness to the qualities of all which surround us, whether two legged or otherwise.

Without proclamation, cloaked with humility and simplicity, these poems are a hymnal that sings gently the parables of how we may find and cherish love—whether in the tat-a-tat-tat of rain falling on an overhead tin roof, the caress of a mountain breeze, the dry, rich smell of sawdust in oh so many stalls, the imagined declaration of a fine old tree, or the expressed affection of a cherished horse's nicker.

If you take deep breaths, be present among all that surrounds you, and allow the music of Kim's words to be vibrant in your own heart, as they are in mine, you will be grateful that you have done so. For just a moment or for a lifetime, you will find serenity. Namaste.

Introduction

The reality of my life has always been far more amazing than even my wildest dreams.

What stories I could share! And, indeed, I have: some of those stories are in the form of poems in this book. I write poetry from the circumstances of my life. Currently, my husband and I live in an old farmhouse with a green tin roof, on seventeen acres in southern Indiana. We have horses, dogs, cats, gardens, a creek that runs through the front pasture, a railroad track that runs along the back. I drew a picture of our farmhouse on a napkin in 1997 when we lived in Arizona, an example for Eric, of the kind of place I wanted to live. We both forgot about it but recognized this farm as home when we drove up the drive here several years later looking to buy a rural property near Louisville, Kentucky. We still have the napkin.

I met Bernadette Spillane, the owner and creator of Happy Dog Ranch, in 2020. I was searching for a miracle, a solution to my plan of training a green-broke six-year-old mustang. I had come to attend a horsemanship clinic with Mark Rashid, a horse trainer I greatly admired. Nothing at that clinic worked out like I had planned. What did happen there at Happy Dog Ranch in that clinic, with Mark and the other instructors, the other clinic participants, and all the people I met, was truly far more amazing than my wildest dreams.

As a way of saying thank you to Happy Dog Ranch, this book is dedicated to Bernadette and John Spillane. And also, to all of the people and animals who come or live, work, teach, volunteer, or in some fashion, find their way to Happy Dog Ranch. The ranch is located in Littleton, Colorado. Miracles happen there, daily. I've been the recipient of more than a few.

One hundred percent of the proceeds from this book go to Happy Dog Ranch, a 501(C3) organization. Some of the poems in this book were written there, written while sitting in our horse trailer looking at the mountains, or sitting near the arena watching people ride and teach, or sitting in sawdust in the stall with my horse, looking out at the expanse of field, fence, folks, and farm animals.

I appreciate you as a reader. Thank you for purchasing this book. May you find a few poems that give you something to think about, or simply that bring a smile.

Kimberly Kaye Esteran
Georgetown, Indiana
2022

LET THE BLIND HORSE LEAD

How Do Trees Decorate Their Toes?
~for Jordan

How do trees decorate their toes?
    With moss and ferns and leaves I suppose.
    And daffodils, violets, wild hyacinth, too.
    And some with pine needles, mushrooms, and flower bells of blue.

Each one is different.
Each its own tree.
Delightful, quite special,
    a wonder to see.
But *seeing* takes time,
one must get up real close—

    To actually see
        how a tree decorates its toes.

I saw a sad sight
    just the other day.
A beautiful tree
    that had no way
to decorate its toes
even though they were there.
This tree's toes were covered with litter,
    tin cans, and even an old spare,
    broken glass, newspapers, beer cans and where

there should have been moss, flowers, and leaves
    I saw only garbage,
        it left me to grieve.

For this tree and its friends
so magnificent and tall
I wondered if they thought Humanity at all:
   Worth a darn?
      Worth a care?
         Worth even a hoot?

I felt pretty bad all the way to my boots.

So, I cleaned up the litter
   threw away all the trash
      and decorated its toes with treasures from my stash.
Like rocks and pinecones, shells, even a note

That said, *"I love trees. And I love you the most!"*
   Don't give up on people.
   Many have good souls.
      And some of us will even
      help decorate your toes.

Today...

Today, I will stop pouring
    myself into the future.

Today, I will open
    and let the future pour into me.

I have read that when things fall apart,
    there is much noise.

But when things come together,
    it is often so quiet, so small,
        we miss it completely.

Today,
    I don't want to miss anything.

Where the Poems Live

Sometimes trying to find
    the words to a poem
        is like looking into a dark cave.

I know they're in there,
    like bats in a barn
        I can hear them rustling

just out of sight.
    Yet they stay hidden
        and the poetry that presents itself

comes in a crooked smile from Grace,
    Jack's brown eyes begging me to play,
        or Billy's soft nicker of recognition.

A more perfect poem
    with better words
        I never could have written.

Isn't It

Isn't it amazing
the word *be*
is in *beautiful*?

And that *loving* and *living*
are different
by only one letter?

And, how wonderful that both
ear and *art*,
are in the word *heart*.

For truly it is an art,
to listen
to the heart ...

... both your own heart
and the hearts
of
others.

Giggle Back to Green

The roses, queens of the garden,
and the peonies, young divas,
open and compete,
or perhaps complement,
this spring garden.

Until one hot day, today,
when it's over,
really over,
they all simultaneously
bow their royal colorful heads,
throw up their lovely, scented flower fingers—
drop everything and
giggle back to green.

A Poem, A Prayer, A Promise

The poem is in the wind
    whispering through the trees,
tossing the flag, sparkling in the creek water,
    playing with the horses' manes and tails.

The prayer is in the pause
    between this action and the next,
this inhale and that exhale, the softness of a smile
    that begins in the heart and moves upward to the eyes.

The promise is in the hands
    that peel potatoes, make the soup,
open and close like birdwings,*
    reach out, touch, offer to help.

*In reference to Rumi's poem *"Birdwings"*

Sacred

Rain on a tin roof.
One drop at a time,
many at once;
soft, soothing,
noisy, wet.
Sacred

Meditation.
One breath in,
one breath out.
Oliver curls by my legs.
Jack stretches by my side.
Grace snores deeply behind me.
All of us
present, together,
mindful, breathing.
Sacred

Life, as it is.
Sorrows and joys.
A river of experience
just like water flowing,
the banks hold it all
but the water shapes
above and below
each side
both banks.
Erosion and flow,
deep and wide,
a journey, this journey.
Sacred

The hole in the clouds
lets blue fall through,
sunlight follows.
Everything glistens,
sundrenched drops of dew descend.
One drop at a time,
many at once;
this place;
old, soothing, noisy, and wet.
Together we live.
Deep and wide.
Necessary.
Sacred

Now

My daily *To Do* list generally
forms itself in one-word instructions:
    Write
    Ride
    Gardens
    Mow
    Stalls
    Walk
    Shelters
    Laundry
    Iron
    Clean ... and so on.
As each action is completed, I cross it off.

The other morning, when I wrote my list for the day,
I inadvertently wrote the word *now*.
Probably meaning to write *mow*,
but I didn't catch it until later.
And then, when I did,
I stopped and looked around at *now*—
this moment, these hands, these dogs,
this sky, this tree, this hawk soaring over me.
And, I thought, *what is now?*
My mind and my heart connected, and I smiled
and realized (again), how precious each moment is.

So, I've added *now* to my daily *To Do* list.
Even yesterday, I added *now* to my grocery list,
curious about what I'd find at the store.
And the gifts I've discovered in those precious
moments of stopping and pausing right *now*—
moments in nature,
smiles from strangers,
my own breath,
sunrise colors,
birdsong,
a fragrance on the wind,
and spaciousness in my own heart—
have been some of the most precious of my days.

Moments I most likely would have missed.
Now, *now* is always on my *To Do* list,
and I never cross it off.
I am learning,
now is more important than anything.

A Little More Rose

Do you ever wonder at the stories of a rose?

Those pale pink ones
growing in my garden
just beside the walk.
When in bloom,
I always pause;
breathe in, breathe out,
their fragrance, their beauty.
They gift me and I become
a little more rose,
a little better me.

And, those other roses,
the ones we found
floating on the water
that South Carolina summer day,
tossed by some bride,
her bouquet a joyful gift to the lake,
or perhaps a bridesmaid's missed catch.
Or perhaps, this bouquet
sent flying in anger,
a proposal or apology vehemently denied.

Their stories a mystery to us,
but still all roses captured in a small net
from our boat.
Gifted to us by children

we placed them in our hair;
water logged, velvet-colored petals,
as we laughingly, wetly, naturally, became
a little more rose
a little better us.

Remember even, the story of fifteen roses—
a friend's story, not my own;
yet roses gifted to each of the fifteen women at the table
with debonair, generosity and panache
as can only happen at a fine dinner in Paris.
Ah, those French!
A single perfect rose
brings out a little more sweetness
of each who receives it.

And, all the other thousand roses,
their stories and fragrances,
colors all their own.
I can only imagine
the affect and effects;
roses sent to a sick one,
or hurt, or gifted in love,
or asking permission,
forgiveness, remembrance,
or simply, the best reason of all,
just because.

Each sweetly fragrant, rose-colored flower
an offering of itself, bringing smiles and beauty.
One little rose,
can change everything.
Just like my pale pink rose
changes me.

How Many Times?
~for Eric

How many times can I write about this place?
The horses, or crows, Jack's brown eyes,
Grace's crooked smile, Oliver or Smoke,
the other barn cats, or Helen, the red-tailed hawk,
the sound of rain on our tin roof,
a single pink rose.

How many times can I look around
and find a balance
between the beauty of what we've created,
and what needs to be done today?

How many times can I raise our flag?
And then lower it once more—
another officer down,
a life of service ending too soon,
leaving family and friends
stunned, in shock, sorrow and surprise.

How many times will my heart
skip a beat when you walk in the door?
Just home from distant lands,
the grocery, walking Jack,
or simply coming in from the barn.

I guess how many times isn't really the question.
Or, if it is, the answer is;
as long as I live, and look, and listen.
As long as I breathe, and write, and love.
Simply put,
as long as I can.

Simple
~in memory of Uno

An inhale and an exhale,
the sweetness of a soft summer breeze.
A pause.

A yellow rose bud at dawn,
an opening at noon,
then fragrance follows in the evening.

The last few breaths in the life of a good dog,
held in loving arms, heart to heart,
moves unafraid and quietly into death.

Your hand holding mine, fingers entwined,
as we walk together on this path
sharing our lives.

A way of being, uncomplicated;
a practice, a lifetime, a journey.
Simple.

Being Present

Being present
to life
is like the blue sky
doing its thing
while the clouds float by.

Sometimes,
I get focused
on the clouds
and completely forget
the blue sky is there.

Too Much Thinking

I'm appropriately masked
sitting in the waiting room
at the car dealership
on the east side of town.
I'm here to get my oil changed.
From where I sit, I can see a small
clump of grass growing up in the rocks
in the otherwise perfectly manicured front garden.

I want to pull it out.

I've been weeding my own gardens at home
for days now and my eyes,
trained for acute weed observation,
and my hands, ready to grip and pull,
spotted this clump just moments
after sitting down.

I'm itching to do something about it.

Is it my internal focus that wants this clump gone?
Is it my chronic need for neatness,
for striving towards perfection?

Am I obsessed with weeds?

If I pulled it out, I'd have to go outside
and get down on my knees,
close to the big ceiling-to-floor front window,
and behind another bush.
I'd be visible to everyone in the waiting room
and those in the upstairs offices.

What would they say?

Maybe, *"Hey lady, nice job!"*
Or, *"Thanks, that clump was really bugging me too."*
More than likely, *"Hey, look at that lady!"*
And, *"What's she doing behind that bush?"*
Continued with, *"Is she okay?"*
Then, *"Maybe she fell?"*
Even, *"Perhaps she's crazy?"*
Finally, *"Wow, maybe she's got Covid?"*
Eventually, someone would call 911.
Or, maybe not?
Maybe the dealership would just refuse to give me service?
Not change the oil in my car?
Ask me to leave?
Then, I'd have to figure out another way to get
to the funeral in Pennsylvania on Wednesday.
Maybe I should change seats in here and
stop looking at that small clump of grass?

Maybe, I'll let someone else weed their garden.

On Grace and Waiting

I tell her *wait*,
and she does.

But, she has a thimbleful
of patience.

And, I often ask
for a quarter cup.

Please. Amen.

Please . . .

Let me be a bridge of kindness,
> a solid place to stand,

a safe way for those crossing troubled times.

Let me be an open ear,
> a holy place of listening

without judgement or criticism.

Let me offer both my hands,
> to hold, hug, steady, or pray.

To bake, to work, and to serve,
open hands that don't grasp.

Let my heart break open
> deeper and wider each day,

offering more compassion, more understanding,
> more patience.

Let me live all the days of my life in this way,
> offering to the world what I have,

offering to the world a little bit of love.

> > > *. . . Amen*

The Practice Before the Practice

The practice before the practice:

*Observing from without,
living and seeing from within.
Listening, before speaking,
intention before striving.
Thoughtful time before expression.
Desire before love.*

I want to hold the string of that kite
and feel the wind in my hands.

I want to ride that horse
and feel the connection through our minds.

I want to surrender to life
and keep practicing all my days.

June, The Month of Perfect Days

June was summer—
    school's out, swimming, suntans, shorts,
        strawberries picked by hand, homemade ice cream,
           campfires, and s'mores.
Can I have another one, please?

June was music— campfire songs . . .
    . . . There's a Hole in the Bucket, B I N G O,
        Going On A Lion Hunt, Row, Row, Row Your Boat . . .
    and concerts, live concerts!
Gosh, I still remember so many!

June is my birth month—
    not just a birthday,
        but a whole month of days
           and then a party, and cake.
Can I have another piece, please?

June was vacation—
    summer camp, band camp, family camping,
        adventures, canoeing, hiking,
           me and Vicki horseback riding.
And, still I ride and still we camp.

June was fireflies, shooting stars, old Western movies, and roses,
    green apples, green tomatoes, gardens and good books,
       TV tag, hide-n-go-seek in the dark,
        and the longest day of the year.
And, halfway to Christmas, certainly another good reason to celebrate!

June is remembering that time goes as fast
    or as slow as one allows.
        A whole month of perfect days.
        June, the month of perfect days.
Can I have another one, please?

One More Thing
~for Jack

Tired. So tired. So very tired.
My body and my mind
this evening
join the generations past, present, and future
of tired ones.
Those who put in a good day's work
and only one more thing
stands between them and bed.

One more thing;
those two brown eyes, hopeful, asking,
a black and white pup,
his little blue ball,
an invitation,
play bow,
a growl and a shake ...

... and we are off on a chase.
Through the living room,
around the chair,
up the stairs and down again,
into the library,
and onto the bed.

Could I disappoint him?
Never.
Could we perhaps stay here, in bed?
Not likely.
And so, 'tis true—
the chase continues and the evening
does as well.

And when, finally,
the lights are off,
the day is done,
the blue ball left in the corner,
and the pup nestles in beside me
curled in the crook of my legs.
I smile in the dark
and am thankful,
deeply thankful,
for that
one
more
thing.

Fresh Mountain Air

The breath is a breeze
blowing across the
mountain meadow of my heart.

Tall grasses and wild flowers
sway gently.
Butterflies, honey bees, and small birds
taste the nectar of secret dreams
and dark fears growing there.

All have found a home.

The Wisdom of a Thousand Years

The feeling in the air is sorrow,
a deep sadness,
irreparable damage.

My eagle feather
and sage, lit and smoking,
my tears, prayers
float up with the smoke.

I walk among the pines
teary-eyed, fanning blessings,
asking forgiveness.

They stand tall,
tall as before,
even with limbs missing,
whole swaths of their bodies gone.

The electric company claims
authority. The air, quiet now,
still smells of oil and machinery
mixed with fresh pine,
and now my sage smoke.

Nothing makes the crows happy.
They curse and cry and caw
from the top of the tallest pine;
one nest, five babies, two angry parents.
They would not leave.
My heart is a long way down.

And yet the pines still offer

new growth, small brown pinecones
budding from end branches.
Each tree holding cut limbs, wreckage,
from its neighbors.

Do they cry?
The sap runs.
Do they feel betrayed?
They stand tall.
Do I want their forgiveness?
Cold, they meet me
like an enemy woman,
guilty by association.

They offer nothing,
but with steadfastness together
remain stoic to the day's events.

The moon will rise,
stars will shine,
the sun as well.
Rain will come,
wind, snow, ice
and even beetles.
The trees will die.
We all die.

But for now, today,
what the pines offer,
what they teach,
is stillness,
and the wisdom of a thousand years.

The Fall

It wasn't just coming off the horse
that hurt.
The fall was simply a culmination
of so many other things
that also hurt.
Things I'd let slip,
or had neglected,
or had just put off
for another time in the future.

Indeed, it was the fall from the horse that
riveted my attention.
All the other little things
had just been omissions,
a letting go by turning away.
Me, ignoring the nagging voices
in my head.
Me, moving too fast
so things couldn't catch up.
Me, just staying busy.

> *Power comes from your center.*
> *Slow your breath, quiet your mind.*

But, they never did go away,
just like the pain in my body now,
it never goes away.
And, funny as it seems,
my doctor tells me I know
exactly how to fix this.
What am I paying him for
anyway?

How many falls will I have
before I change my trajectory?
How many voices in my head,
talking, talking, talking,
before I get quiet and listen
to the *one Voice* that matters?
How many excuses?

> *Where* is my ground?
> What *is* my name?
> Where is *my* teacher?
> Who is my *next horse?*

Summer Solstice
~at Happy Dog Ranch

The clouds, dark grey and brooding,
determinedly move forward
pulling night with them,
cloaking the stars,
flowing over the mountains in the west,
shrouding everything in wetness.

The rain follows—
sound first moving across the land,
then water, as everything succumbs
to the dark and heavy downpour.
Grasses, horses, people,
all bow down, turn tail to the wind,
hurry to find shelter.

And it comes,
darkness and a steady downpour
pulled by a strong wind.
The whole horizon closes in to grey
then black.

Puddles get larger, mud deeper.
The sound is deafening—
we listen from our bed, tossing and turning;
worry about things we have no control over;

fall sleep; dream crazy dreams; wake up.
And then it's gone.

Gone, in the early morning dawn,
colors of pink, gold, and baby blues
tint the soft sky in ever changing hues
leaving only freshness and light,
clear light, reflecting upward to clear blue,
cleansed and cool.

This morning as I feed the horses
and move through my chores
it seems as if God plays in the puddles, grasses,
manes, and tails.
People smile and squish through mud,
share stories, splash.
Laughter, like light, floats upward.

Day Three

I.
"There are a lot of holes in his learning.
He's still a really good horse.
But, he's not a good horse for you."
    ~Mark

"Integrity is doing the right thing,
even when no one is looking.
Perhaps, especially, when no one is looking."
    ~Kim

II.
I've been crying a lot lately.
Perhaps, beginning tomorrow
I won't feel the need to cry?
Perhaps, beginning tomorrow
I can begin working on my horsemanship skills?
Perhaps, beginning tomorrow,
I can become a "horse rider" and not a "horse owner"?
Perhaps, beginning right now,
things will begin to flow?

"Perhaps" holds a lot of potential.

III.
Today, I have begun letting Jasper go.
    He will stay here.
His fate is bigger than what
        I can imagine.
Someone will have an awesome horse in him
        I will someday have an awesome horse of my own.

Life works and flows as long
    as I am willing to work and flow, too.
That one lesson seems to be
    repeating itself over and over again.

I'm getting a little closer to understanding.

> *Miracle stories: Jasper did stay at Happy Dog Ranch. Bernadette had room for him to be boarded. Gray trained him for 90 days. During that time, Jasper was also used as a demonstration horse by Jim Masterson during the Brain Clinic presented at Happy Dog Ranch later that summer. At that clinic, a woman, Rebecca, also a client and friend of Gray's, fell in love with Jasper and eventually purchased him. Jasper is now living just outside, Denver, Co, at Renewing Hope Ranch, where he is a therapy horse and works in their First Responders and Veteran Program. Please check out their website to learn more about their program and the miracle of equine-assisted therapy, renewinghoperanch.org.*

Stones and Tears

The small round stone
    in my pocket
        was a mountain at one time.

Just like the tears
    in my eyes
        once belonged to my heart.

Holding Up a Mountain
~for Mark

Holding up a mountain.
   Not breathing.

Running down a mountain.
   Hell bent.
      Leather.

The wind pursues
   with stories from the past;
all the while, the sun
      beats bright light
         into me as Truth.

And, perhaps they were.
   Stories true then, but not now.

Now the Truth asks me to stop holding on;
   open the hands,
   open the mind,
   open the heart.
      Listen.

Start breathing.
    Feel the mountain air.
Stop running.
    There is a still, quiet place within.
Listen closely.
    Someone is whispering something,
        something about a miracle.

> *I wrote this poem the day Mark told me that*
> *my mustang, Jasper, was a good horse, just not*
> *a good horse for me.*
> *So much has happened since that day.*
> *But doesn't everything always happen anyway?*
> *It's only when we start breathing, stop running,*
> *and start listening do we ever really hear.*

Energy

The thing about energy
is that it is always best
when gathered to your center
and then given away.
Gather again, and give.

Repeat...

Thus, one gets filled and emptied
with each gathering and giving.
This is like the ocean
and like the breath.

This is also how love works.

A Daily Reminder

The full moon, whole and round,
... settles softly behind the mountains,
the last top curve reflecting gold
from the morning sun.

This path of rising and setting,
reflecting and glowing,
from these two ancient orbs
as they move across the sky
are a reminder for me
to walk my own path,
and to reflect back to others
their light and also to be still long enough
to see my reflection from theirs.

There is a rhythm to the rising and setting,
a beautiful light and a mysterious dark,
this ebb and flow held in each of us.
This moon and this sun, a daily reminder
to see and be seen,
to reflect and be filled,
to ebb and to flow,
to slow down and be a part of the whole.

The Knife

It appeared quite suddenly,
the knife.
Pulled from his pocket,
held in his working hands
softly, glinting in the sunlight.

An example, can you see?

Simply a sudden turn of events,
a new perspective;
this sharp blade.

Like a line,
how thin can this line be?
How long?
Life and death,
worlds apart, yet
paper thin,
one side or the other,
so close, or so far.

Stop and pay attention,
blunt or sharp,
it always depends.
Can you see the songbird
turn to song?

Can you trace the path
of movement in your body first?
Can you feel the horse become
your legs? Your breath? Your heart?
Can you feel, but not control,
guide, remain soft?
Connect, yet still lead?

*The blunt side teaches lessons
only the humble can accept.*

Life gives what it gives and takes equally.
There is no score.
This place is sacred,
offering time to listen deeply,
yet not to settle.
Time to practice reverence and
self-inquiry,
yet not preoccupation.
Time to change the internal dialog,
quiet the cynic,
and yet,
not become sidetracked
by other voices.

I can see clearly, where I am.
And so, what now?
What now,
indeed.

Softly
~for Crissi

I.
"Softly?" he questions.
"Yes, softly," I answer.
"But, I've never done it softly," he says hesitantly.
"That's okay. We can do it together," I reply.
"Okay, I suppose," and he lowers his head.

I gently fasten the halter and pick up the lead rope.
Pause.
Ask him to join me,
then open the gate.
Softly.

II.
How you pick up a coffee cup,
answer a question,
pet the dog,
breathe,
ride a horse . . .

Softness doesn't mean passive.
Softness means *a joining with* and then using
the least amount of pressure necessary,
the least amount of pressure possible.
Softness isn't trading out your inside
for an outside expectation.

To be soft with anything,
one needs to be very, very
connected.

Count By Touching
~for Jessica

What are the qualities of a wild heart?
Like a hawk that soars without effort,
or a bee intoxicated by lavender honey,
even as a single drop of dew reflects the whole world,
with tenderness and patience, these qualities abide:
to dream, to wait, to act,
to move, to live.
To live from the heart, compassionately.

> *Wild hearts dance and sing*
> *Wild hearts whisper and dream*
> *Wild hearts abide in tenderness*
> *Wild hearts count by touching*

Where does a wild heart grow?
In mountains, cities, and small towns,
on farms, or sanctuaries, down an old country road.
It grows in fields of flowers.
The wild heart circles around,
like the seasons, or the days and nights

in clear skies or those filled with clouds.
It plays in waters, flowing wild and deep,
or rests in ponds fed with underground springs.

> *Wild hearts dance and sing*
> *Wild hearts whisper and dream*
> *Wild hearts abide in tenderness*
> *Wild hearts count by touching*

What does a wild heart need?
A wild heart needs only a dream,
some space, a place to open its wings,
and then, perhaps, some time to organize things.
A wild heart can be found just about anywhere.
It's often improbable, never impossible.
You'll know it when you see it.
It may make you blush, or pause,
take a breath or smile.
It might even encourage your own heart
to dance and sing, whisper or dream.
Wild hearts are contagious.
Be careful.
Wild hearts count by touching.

Good-bye Stories

And, in our own way
    we have joined the age-old river
of grief and good-byes
    that flows through
        every life.

The hollowness of heart,
    with a depth and bottom until now unknown
where only pure water, fresh air, and time
    can wash smooth
        the edges of our sadness.

Water, time, and tears,
    and our willingness to move on;
to go together into unchartered lands,
    carrying our good-bye stories
        close in our hearts.

Open My Mind

Open my mind
    farther than the most distant horizon.

Open my heart wider
    than the darkest, blackest star-studded sky.

Deepen my understanding
    to realms beyond my wildest imagination.

Keep me present to each moment
    like the pine tree stays present to the breeze.

Cookies
~for Czar Mir
May 5, 1999-July 4, 2019

I ask the white horse to trust me,
    he asks the same of me.

I ask the white horse to listen,
    he requests the same respect.

I ask the white horse to learn
    my body language and respond.
        He says, *"Ditto. Same to you."*

I ask the white horse to carry me.
    He says, "Get on. Be clear."

I ask the white horse if he wants a cookie?
    He says, "What took you so long
        to read my mind?"

The Apple Tree

If she cried out, I did not hear.
The sound of the rain
was heavy and loud.

The weight of her fruit,
green jewels hanging from her limbs,
must have become unbearable.

Surely there was a cry?
An anguished sound,
as a thick prominent limb

ripped down and away from her trunk,
crashing to earth amidst
the already fierce and deafening storm.

It had to hurt.
Had to be traumatic.
And yet, when I found her

bedraggled in the bright sunlight—
me, out looking for rainbows
after the storm—

there she stood:
proud, stoic, glistening, green, and beautiful.
Raising up her few remaining limbs

as if to say,
"Yes, I am here."
"Yes, there is damage."

"Yes, there is a rainbow,
and I have been standing here in full color
watching it grow."

Griffin Dreams

I am a small griffin,
wings of gossamer,
lion's paws,
soft of eye.

I listen to the language of the night,
dreams and prayers unspoken,
small feet on leaves and grasses,
wind song sighing on high,
soft creek sounds dancing over stones and mosses.

My adornments are quite simple:
a single strand of pearls,
gifts of my mother;
a single ring of gold,
forged and melted from
deep in the sacred mountain.

I eat moon drops and lavender petals,
and sometimes blueberries coated in mist.
My thirst is quenched
from morning dew gathered in
the small cups of flowers.

My only desire is to present for you
the magic of this otherworld;
nighttime mystics and mysteries,
once removed from Bluetooth phones
and computer updates,
busy schedules, and
too much thinking.

You presume I hide,
but I am always here,
present in the leaves of the trees,
luminescent in the clouds,
mixed in with the colors of the rainbow.
To find me, you need only to remain open,
slow down,
and see without looking,
hear without listening,
love without needing.

Although I travel solo
I am never alone.
The Circle of Life connects me with all,
and the common language we speak is Love.
You will understand this, too,
when you pause and listen with your heart.

I was on my way to the seashore,
but stopped in to say hello.
A light kiss on your cheek,
the whisper of my wings
in your ears,
and the tiny door behind the
school house in your dreams
let me in and out;
like a fragrance,
like a blessing,
like a memory
of a once forgotten song.

Long and Deep

Home at last, a month on the road,
    and the list is long and deep.

Long, like the grass and the weeds in the gardens.
    Deep, like the leftover hay and manure in the dry lots.

Long, like the list of things
    we each have in our minds of *things to be done now.*
Deep, like our hearts with thoughts of
    horses left behind, and what lies ahead.

But, Jack and Grace have other plans:

    "Come play!" they say, eyes bright, tails wagging.
    "Let's play in the creek and search for crawdads
        and you can throw sticks."
    "It's not too deep and won't take too long."

Our dogs are so wise.

Vitality

Lean in.
Listen with your heart.
See through the lens of intuition
how all things are interconnected,
how the vitality of life
is always present.

Watch closely.
The green maple leaf
high up in the tree is listening
to the songs from the Earth
and preparing to burst into
bright red flame.

secrets

secrets
are heavy
invisible weights
on words and shoulders
alert guardians of conversations
and already too little sleep
rusty and creaky catches
on the latches
of the heart

secrets
are never secret
in the ever-constant conversation
between the many
voices in our
head

Thoughts on Surrender

Nothing has ever gone exactly as I planned, thankfully.
Resistance was futile, but gave me strength to holdfast.
Will, like a strong wind, blew me in a direction
so that I grew like a leeward tree, bent by the wind.
When surrender finally came, with it also
came a softening, a form of grace.

With surrender sometimes I felt lost;
my boundaries diminished,
the space was different.
Reorganization vital.
Yet there, in that space of groundlessness
I found pieces of myself—

wise and creative, flexible, grateful,
strong and humble
and claimed them as my own.
Sometimes it took a long time.
Eventually, gratitude followed and I could say, *"Thank you."*
Thank you for everything that has brought me to this place
in life.

And that, too, has often taken a very long time.

There Is a Sweetness in an Old Dog's Joy
~for Grace, with love

There is a sweetness in an old dog's joy.
The deep shine of the eyes,
the slow wag of the tail,
the happy open smile.

Our girl, Grace, will soon be 11,
or maybe older, we don't know.
I found her in the woods.
Found her and her pup, Jack,
ten years ago.

Grace loves me, and she shows it.
Daily.
She shares her smile,
her enthusiasm for life,
or napping,
or peanut butter,
or, just being loved.

When she can't find me, she goes looking.
The familiar places first:
bedroom, kitchen, laundry room,
yoga room, front porch, office.
Or, in the Spring,
around the house, then in the gardens.

Gradually, her searching spirals outward,
eventually reaching the barn.
She always finds me.

Her eyes have cataracts
and her hearing is fading.
Yet, she still follows me to the barn,
around the pasture;
plays with stuffed toys in the morning;
sleeps, and snores deeply,
sometimes on my yoga mat upstairs,
almost always when I meditate.

She is happy, I feel it.
When we go out for walks,
she hesitates when I get too far ahead,
so I turn around and jump.
Yes, jump... up and down,
and wave my arms,
so she can see me.
It always makes me laugh out loud,
being silly for her.
But then,
with a wag of her tail
and that beautiful smile,
she runs to me and we continue.

Yes, there is a great deal of sweetness
in our old dog's joy.

Walking Trees
~for Jill, who knows

The wind sings through the woods
    from high on the ridge sinking into the valley;
pushing grasses, pulling leaves, slapping limbs,
    Nature's jaunty jazz band captures the heart, awakens
the senses.

The water from the Blue River,
    constant in its flowing through time,
draws the wind, leaves, limbs,
    and all beings to its rocky shore.

There sunlight glitters above still picturesque reflections
    while rapids, white and rushing,
flow beyond the blue-green depths—
    capture the eye, stop the breath, engage the heart;
offer treasures to be found in hand and memory.

All of us come to find respite here,
    nourishment for body and soul,
a kinship with all beings,
    a source for solace.

And, in one magical place
    even the trees appear to tiptoe
high on long roots, windblown, yet tall,
    slowly moving toward the river.

In Your Eyes
~for Eric

In your eyes, I see the reflection
    of the woman I long to be.

In your heart, I am wrapped in love
    beyond my wildest dreams.

In your arms, I find comfort
    when the whole world is in a state of chaos.

In sharing your life, my soul
    sings with joy and in harmony with yours.

In quiet gratitude and love, I watch you sleep
    and my heart breaks open once more.

And This . . .
~in memory of Perrie

The messiness about being human
stuns me into stillness.
Pain, change, journey, and joy . . .
all paths lead from the past to the future.
We stand in the middle,
both forward and back,
being brought here by walking,
one step, one day, one year
at a time.

We cannot face only one direction and
praise upward or curse below.
All directions hold us in balance,
or hold us crooked.

Yet, still we are held.

And any time we are standing,
breathing, laughing,
present, crying, numb,
we are walking this path.
We are living,
whether slow or fast,
right side or upside
down.

Riots, insurrections, pandemics,
hope, praise, cancer, or fear,
all things are an illusion.
Yet, all things,
like the moon and morning star,
are real in this moment.
And what are we
at our very best,
if not solely here, right here,
in this very moment?

Being human today —
feeling that magic when one moment unfolds
into another moment;
where truth
lies at the bottom of your heart
or your feet,
or somewhere in between.

Can we stand and say,
I am here. Please hold me.

Then ask:
What is despairing?
Where is hope?
Who am I?
And, once more,
begin again.

We are praying people.
We can see the stars.
Someone dies.
We love.
We cry.

Musings from the Stall
~for Sarah

I've spent a lot of time in sawdust,
sitting on a stall floor.
As a kid, it's where I did my homework.
A little later, it's where I got my first kiss,
and a bit later, drank my first beer.

But lately it has also been the place
I watched and waited.
Watched and tended injuries,
knees, feet, hocks, eyes . . .
Waited for a settling, a softening,
a change, a calm, a sign.

And while I've not had a horse die
in a stall,
I've had several horses, in the days
just before dying
lay with me,
both of us nestled in sawdust,
eyes closed, breathing labored,
hearts joined.

Those moments of waiting,
poignant in their solitude and generosity,
mystical in the sharing
of breath and space
between one horse, one woman;
two hearts, two lives;
one quiet moment.

Those moments have changed me.
Each horse changes me.
And, for every time I sit in a stall,
covered in sawdust,
I am reminded that being present
to this moment, right now:
this horse, this journey,
no matter the outcome.
This is the greatest gift of all.

I Didn't Know

I didn't know that until I fell a thousand times,
    I could also put myself back together.

I didn't know that when I gifted flowers, poems,
    bread, cookies, time, and listening,
    that I was living my truth in kindness.

I didn't know that when I am on my knees
    in the garden, praying and pulling weeds,
    throwing dirt clods for Jack,
    loving Grace nose-to-nose, and tending flowers
    that I was being authentically me.

I didn't know that for every kindness
    I've ever offered another, I've added
    a precious hour to my time here on Earth.

I didn't know that I'm already who I am
    and always have been. And that life,
    like water over a stone, has been gently
    and steadily wearing my edges smooth.

And, even though I didn't know these things,
    and many more, today I am content
    to be me and wander authentically
    with kindness and patience,
    listening and loving the world
    into the wide-open spaces
    of not knowing.

Tough

We are strong.
We are determined.
We show up.
We care.

We work hard.
We sweat.
We dream.
We share.

We can do many things
that are hard, that take some planning,
that require commitment,
some tenacity to prevail.

But the toughest breath
I can ever imagine,
will be the inhale
after the other's last exhale.

These Words

"Some things just take a little time."
"You can't push a river."
"You'll know."
"Many hands make light work."
"Take what we have and split it in half,
 it will be enough."
"Let us pray."

These words
all of them gifts,
lessons and teachings
from the people of my past.

These words
remind me how to be
when I'm searching
for what truly matters.

These words
remind me that
who I am
is more than enough.

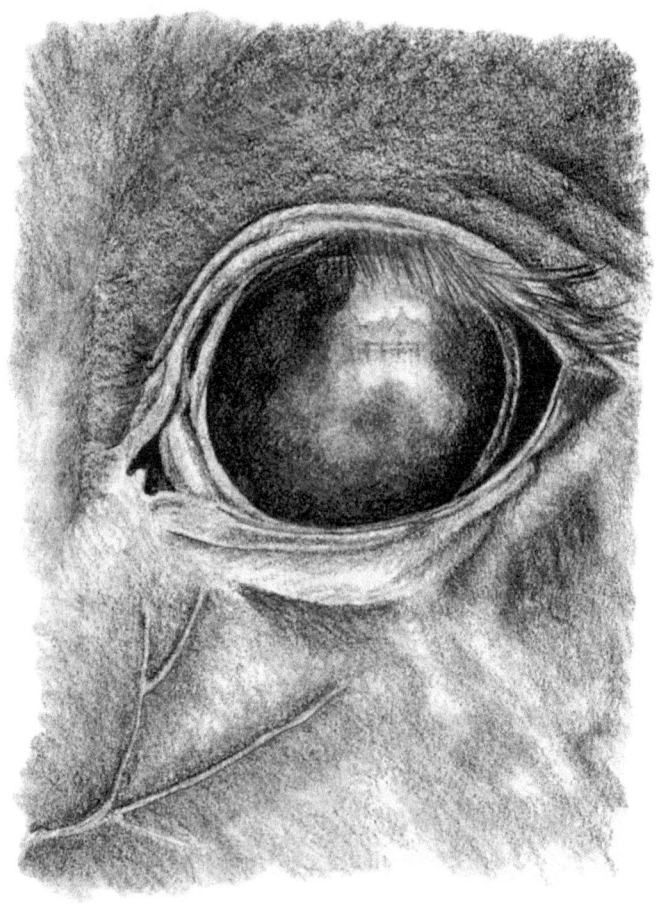

Let the Blind Horse Lead

Billy. He's a Quarter Horse, a big blue roan.
Handsome. Everyone says so.
He is somewhere between the age of 13 and 20;
we don't know for sure, and it really doesn't matter.

He came to us a year ago from South Dakota,
but his origins are in Wyoming. He was a ranch horse.
I bet he was a darn good one, too.
I'm quite sure he knows more about ranching
than I ever will. He's seen things, been there.
He's patient, smart, willing, strong.
He is kind.
He's also blind.

Yet, Billy and I trail ride, do obstacle courses,
participate in clinics, even work cows.
We also visit residents at nursing homes
and independent living facilities.
He lets people in wheelchairs touch his face,
pet him, tell him their stories and their fears.
We listen a lot.

When other horses, whether young or inexperienced,
have an issue on the trail, in a spooky spot,
or with uncertainty, Billy always steps in,
calmly, with the sureness of a Zen master,
to lead the way. We laugh and say,
"Let the blind horse lead," and he does.

Billy teaches me and others about faith,
hope, and love. About life in the present moment.
And, most importantly, about trust.
Billy isn't necessarily the horse I wanted,
but Billy is most certainly the horse I needed.
I am his eyes, his guide.
He is my horse, my teacher.
Together, we're having some incredible adventures.

Oh yes, let the blind horse lead!

Scatter Me

Scatter me in a high mountain meadow
    where I can be part of the wild flowers blooming,
where bear paws and elk hooves
    can track me into the forest.

Scatter me under tall white pines
    where I can hear blue jays quarrel and eagles call,
be found by sticky squirrel feet
    and taken up into the high green heights.

Scatter me in a clear mountain stream
    where I can float downward in a cold wet rush
over rocks and roots, and soar daringly over waterfalls
    singing in harmony with the watery mountain music.

Scatter me here, and, if I am lucky
    I will sink to the stream bottom,
mingle with dirt and rocks, leaves and bones,
    and eventually turn to stone.

And then, in 10,000 years or more
    someone will find me—
small and round, polished and whole once again—
    pick me up, and tuck me in their pocket.

Epilogue

Listening to the Horses

Three horses in Southern Indiana stand nose to tail in the shade of a big maple tree. The hot August sun bakes the ground beneath their feet. Heat shimmers in the air. The only movement is the occasional swish of a tail. The only sound, the low buzz of a fly and the distant hum from the radio in the barn.

Or is it? Listen closer:

"A piano? Really?" the bay horse questions.
"Yes, a piano," the white horse replies.
"In the street?"
"Yes, in the street."
"What kind of music?" inquires the black horse doubtfully.
"Never mind what kind of music! Where and why?" interrupts the bay, stamping his foot.
"Well, classical and folk, that was the music. At a refugee camp in Syria, a Palestinian refugee camp in Syria," the white horse explained quietly.
"Because guns don't work. That's what they said," he added.
"What happened then?" asked the black horse.
"Only the children came out. Everyone else was afraid," the white horse answered.
"But the children came?" asked the bay, shaking his head and stamping his foot again.
"Yes, the children came out into the streets and smiled."
"They smiled?"

"Yes."

"Perhaps there is more hope for peace than we thought?" suggested the black horse.

"Perhaps," the white horse responded, and then added, *"It depends upon the children."*

"Yes, the children know. The children always know," said the black horse wisely.

And the three horses—the white, the bay, and the black—nodded their heads, yawned, and blinked slowly, and remained standing in the shade of the old maple tree. And, the sun was hot, and the heat shimmered in the air. And, the only sound was the sound of the flies buzzing and now, music coming from the open barn door. The only movements, the occasional swish of a tail and the stamp of a foot.

Dedicated to Ayham Ahmad, the Pianist of Yarmouk, in the refugee camp. I heard this story on NPR while I was working in the barn, the horses standing nearby, and I imagined the horses hearing it also. And hearing it in their infinite wisdom of "horse-ness" and being able to see through the politics and all the other stuff that complicates life. How they might "hear" things differently and perhaps, a bit more wisely than we do.

With Gratitude

I offer my deepest gratitude to all the people who have believed in me and supported me on this journey. The old saying, "*It takes a village*" is true of many things: raising children, horses, dogs, creating gardens, dreams, and books. This book wouldn't be possible without the support and assistance of many people.

First, I offer my love and gratitude to my husband Eric, for always believing in me. This life and this love we share is indeed its own miracle. An immense amount of love and thanks to my niece, Jordan Davis, who is the very talented illustrator for this book. When I asked her to consider doing the artwork, I knew then she was one very busy lady; wife, mother, teacher, *and* in the process of building a new home. Yet, she said yes. Thank you, Jordan! Your talents and creative gifts make this book far more than I ever dreamed. Thank you to my dear friend, Jeffrey Ritter, for writing the Forward. You have known me for a very, very long time. Your friendship, like the words you wrote, is precious to my heart. Gratitude and love to Jane Kuhar for editing these poems and offering her sense of flow, grammar, and observations in the most kind, delightful, and helpful ways. I *love* working with you! A heartfelt gratitude to Crissi McDonald, co-owner of Lilith House Press, for her encouragement and belief that my voice, my words, my poems, had a special place in this world. And, for introducing me to Lilith House Press, their amazing support in getting this book into print and into your hands has yet again, been miraculous. To Bernadette and John Spillane and the Happy Dog Ranch Family, you change lives, you changed mine. And, a deep heartfelt gratitude to Gray Kyle-Graves, you are awesome! Thank you for everything, but specifically for saying *"yes"* without hesitation, to work with Jasper. And then, for everything else that followed. Love and appreciation to you.

And, to my family and my friends who have received poems, listened to my dreams, and shared in my ups and downs and all the in-between places. You are each precious to my life. You may not be mentioned by name here, but you are in many of the poems; we've hiked, boated, and camped, Google Duo'ed and Zoomed together, sat under trees and meditated, practiced yoga, picnicked, talked on porches, in kitchens, decks and in barns, laid with horses out in pastures, fallen apart, cried and listened each other whole again. You are *always* in my heart. If you've ever read these next words in a note, letter or card from me, I am talking about you. *So much love comes from here!*

And lastly, my heart and love to the dogs, horses, and cats that have shared my life. I can't even begin to imagine where I would be or what life would be without you.

Kimberly Kaye Esteran
2022

About the Author

Kimberly Esteran lives with her husband Eric, their two dogs, four horses, and seven cats in an old yellow farmhouse with a green tin roof on seventeen acres in Southern Indiana. She loves writing poetry and riding horses, training their dogs, gardening, and music. Yoga and meditation, cooking with her husband, and long walks in the woods keep her content, creative, and curious about life. *Let the Blind Horse Lead* is her third book of poetry, and the first book she has co-created with her niece, Jordan Davis.

Photo by Eric Esteran

Also available as an ebook.

About the Illustrator

Jordan Davis is a self-taught artist with *Let the Blind Horse Lead* her debut project. She enjoys creating realistic art with pencil or charcoal. In her spare time, Jordan enjoys traveling and exploring new places. She is a special education teacher in Central Ohio where she lives with her husband Ted and their three children.

Photo by Mark Richards

www.ingramcontent.com/pod-product-compliance
Lightning Source LLC
Chambersburg PA
CBHW020301030426
42336CB00010B/851